Eleven Wonders

Julia Deakin

graft
poetry

2012

Published 2012

Graft Poetry
Frizingley Hall
Frizinghall Road
Bradford BD9 4LD
West Yorkshire

www.graftpoetry.co.uk

Printed by Inprint + Design, Bradford
Cover design: www.cloudspotting.co.uk and Julia Deakin

ISBN 978-0-9558400-5-0

ACKNOWLEDGEMENTS

Thanks are due to editors of the following, who first published some of these poems: *Aesthetica Creative Works Annual 2010, Acumen, www.barehandspoetry.com, The Bridport Prize Annual 2011, Battered Moons Competition Booklet 2012, Brittle Star, Best of Manchester Poets Vols I & II, Envoi, Grist, www.imaginingstaffordshire.org.uk, Obsessed with Pipework, Pennine Platform, Poetry London, Raw Edge* and *The Yorkshire Post.* 'Personal Effects' won the Yorkshire Open Poetry Competition 2010, 'Exceedingly good cakes' the Torriano Poetry Competition 2011, 'Crabtree to Gascoigne, 1641' the LIPPfest Competition 2011, 'Pupil' the Elmet Competition 2011 and 'Play' the Bare Hands International Competition 2012.

CONTENTS

Nameless

Kingfisher on a tram

Play

Nameless

Slice

Before they built this terrace in the 1870s
they kept pigs on this patch of land,
the owner big in butchery, whose shop
on Harehills Road fed servants
from the big houses Moortown way, and
non-observant Jewish garment workers.

Hard to picture, here, where the row has stood
a century and seen off several tenants' decors,
that beneath the carpeted front parlour and above
the level of the cellar set-pot, the soil
these were dug from sustained pigs, the ground worn
to the precise consistency pigs like, to feel at home.

It's built up now and traffic-bound, the only trace
of 'Woodland View' a few park trees. Evenings,
in our dark green papered living room
with its bay window seat and art nouveau
tiled fireplace, we listen, between sputters
from the frosty little gas fire, for the snuffling.

Personal effects
Haddon Hall, Derbyshire

What haunts after all is not the brass neck of the place
but in a side room, underlit, flung out from the hub,
spirited through cracks between floorboards and flags
to lie cached like exhibits for some overdue case:

the lost keys and coins, washing tallies, playing cards;
a three-inch Christ crucified, minus its cross.
Lodged behind panels near the great fireplace,
the portrait of a young lady holding a small dog.

A bottle by the staircase up to Roger Manners' room;
a buckle, a hat ornament, a faceted glass stem.
A Papal lead bulla found while cutting a trench;
a horn book; portions of a stringed instrument.

A candle snuffer, letter seals, a child's leather shoe;
an Edward VI shilling wedged beneath a chapel pew;
a turned dolls' house table leg; nail scissors, pins;
two ivory nozzles of a vaginal syringe.

And out from behind these the tired skin and bone
of the last hands to touch them before letting go –
the apprentice, the pot boy, the pale governess,
the world-weary valet, the tense paying guest.

From the guts of the whale that swallowed them whole
through the racetrack of sculleries, backstairs and halls,
past the cold chapel frescoes of monochrome flowers
sucking up to the window like dutiful souls,

down the rose-studded gardens and sinuous drive
hear their calloused feet thunder, their anthem gain pace
as reclaiming the shreds of their shadowy lives
they stride with their visitors out of the gate.

Crabtree to Gascoigne, 1641

So, our dear Horrocks is gone. Twenty-two. I must repeat
what I find so hard to accept: that such a bright star
should be lost to us so young. After all we shared,
I shall never now shake his hand.

That November Sunday he, the better astronomer,
noted his observations there and then. I was too overcome
to touch a pen. I shall make amends.

Tonight though, at my window, the cosmos
he proved vaster and more ordered than we thought
seems emptier – a mere expanse.

My lenses mist.

Would he have planned to visit had he felt unwell,
or been ill for long? No, he was in health for all we knew.

Which, in the end, was what? Something of the spheres,
their transit centuries hence. But of tomorrow –
of accidents round corners, stalking maladies, guests
with knives – nothing. Nothing about our inner storms
or numbered days. More of the heavenly bodies
than of ours.

Thus I am plagued by fears: that to fathom the skies
without first grasping our own profound cosmologies
is perverse. That to see – not as prophets but mathematicians,
the year, the day, the hour – so far ahead, is to spy
on God.

These fears I want his reason to reject.

But since my telescope cannot bring him closer,
it leaves me cold. I have no heart for work. No instrument,
good Sir, to measure loss.

Jeremiah Horrocks [1619-1641] first recorded the transit of Venus and predicted future transits, including 8th June 2004. 'The Keats of English astronomy' died the day before he was to meet his mentee William Crabtree [1610-1644]. Their friend William Gascoigne of Leeds [1612-1644] invented the micrometer.

Nameless

Those last weeks, you dragged yourself
up to the landing window, one or other of us with you,
to crane up at the sky's edge.

No astronomer, you knew no constellations
any more than I do – though I still hope
to learn.

So every black expanse
looked much the same, though no less wonderful
for being unnamed.

But this   creature   trailing fire and ice
was something else. You could tell it from the rest
and yes, it seemed portentous – that word for it
came straight away. It was going somewhere
slowly, unstoppably and marvellously.

Silenced by your silence we sat, staring.
We all understood.

After Rothko
Black on grey, 1969

This is not the night sky, teeming with more than we know.
This is not the abyss. Not a black hole. Not unremitting black.
This is not a compulsion to make something out of nothing.
This is not nihilism, nor existentialism. This is not the choice.
This is not our future, not our past, not the next step. This is
not the frontier of human understanding. This is not infinity.
This is not the dawn of creation, nor its end. This is not the
consequence of vaunting ambition. This is not an astronaut's
vision nor a transfixed audience's nightly television. This is
not the science of proportion. This is not the state of this world
as we leave it for others. This is not tragic. This is not the edge.
This is not a slight curvature. This
is not the shape of every planet in
existence. This is not featureless
grey. Not a moonscape. Not
scorched earth. Not ruined
Manhattan. Not a runway. Not a
victim's last view. Not cold war. Not
depression. Not the colour of
thought. It is paint on paper. It is just

- 15 -

Prayer

you
have done
this before – slipped
your unclothed limbs
into these shallows – left baggage
on the shore – wished it stolen
as you have stolen away –
have made your body a boat
and let it float – let the rope slither
and sink – have let yourself drift, oarless
into mist – against broken objects,
shared their fate – let light fade,
waves take your weight –
felt yourself sinking and half said
don't wake me, day, let me loose –
let me lose myself – life, let me
go – night after night
you have trusted
so why not
now

Queen of the Inch
Rothesay Museum: Inchmarnock Bronze Age knife and necklace

On the far side of an island off an island
      in a time before the time before our time,
a family laid to rest their stricken daughter
      by the winding sheet of water where she died.

They wrapped her in her finest cloak and collar
      and closed her fingers round her trapping knife,
and with the things she treasured most about her
      tucked up their ashen princess for the night.

The tomb they set her in was made of granite,
      its quarrying begun before her birth.
Her lover and her kinsmen had worked on it,
      not dreaming that one day it would be hers.

The kist's construction was proclaimed a wonder –
      its chiselled rebate brought the island fame.
But still they felt the press of stone upon her –
      the pitiless assault of wind and rain.

They knew how winter's icy club would shatter,
      how harshly summer's rays would penetrate.
They knew how soon the collar's thread would scatter
      black beads among the whiter vertebrae.

Was such a lavish grave, then, just a prison?
      What of the cap stone fitting into place?
Might not what had slid on with such precision
      as magically, too, be slid away?

They dreamed and woke and fed upon this vision
　　　as if, when she had simply outslept death,
she might rise up and, finding strength god-given,
　　　step out to taste the spring breeze on her breath

and drinking in the 'wide and lovely view'[1] there
　　　sweeping from the mist-tipped northern Kyles
down to Kilmory in the west, might let the sea air
　　　stir her appetite, revive her trapping skills

and when she'd eaten, feast her mind at length
　　　on firelit faces, love, the salt-smoke taste of skin,
warm flesh on flesh, the dual strength
　　　of interlocking arms, the pride of winning

and of being won, of wearing triumph:
　　　sun and stars in lignite beads entwined
and multiplying, like a blood alliance.
　　　This was the hope that dawned on their horizon,

the thread drawn out to offer consolation,
　　　the beads of story added year by year
until, some fifteen-hundred winters later,
　　　they held the circle up and saw a prayer.

As if the chiselled secret of the tomb meant
　　　their child might one day choose to be reborn.
As if, when their time came, they too might walk free,
　　　as easily as opening a door.

[1] Marshall, D. (1903) *The "Queen of the Inch"* – Museum Archive

Scarface
Flockton Moor, West Yorkshire

This landscape is hand-made – an artefact
hacked up and stitched together bit by bit:
each slap of mortar, brick and lick of pointing,
plumb-lined chimney stack, each post, each tile,
once chosen from the pile, eclipsed the world
just long enough, until aligned and set in place
to hold some farm hand's breath an instant,
critically.

That row of trees: each had their moment, too,
as saplings, chosen, planted, spaced and watered in;
again, a held breath checking the earth's axis
momentarily. Even the hollows on that hillside
trace the lines of ancient mine shafts, worked out
blow by blow, inch by breathless inch –
which only the hands of wind and rain
now rearrange.

Possession

(On revisiting a second-hand copy of Adcock's *Twentieth Century Women's Poetry* signed in green felt-tip *Elizabeth Scully* or *Scally, Hebden Bridge)*

It falls open first at Plath then Adrienne Rich,
the sections between flapping back and forth at me
in virginal blocks. Spinster and Lady Lazarus
have been scribbled on or 'annotated' in the same heavy hand,
a pencil as thick as the pen.

Well it's mine now, Elizabeth Scally or Scully, so I get a rubber,
clamp the page under my left arm and rub out *1962,*
a line from Spinster to girl, *universal, cultural position of women,*
a ring round *Nazi lampshade, promise of feminine empowerment,*
AND THAT'S ALL SHE IS, make them pay, in control of the image
and some kind of plumbing diagram round *Out of ash I rise.*

Now, Adrienne: *focus is now on the woman in the poems,*
three strange Masonic triangles, *waster,* and *cf Baudelaire or TWL.*

Next, break the spine at Mew, Bishop, Cope, Rukeyser, Guest –
Plath by now of course falling apart – and *read* some.
Let's hear it for them. And Eiléan Ni Chuilleanáin,
whom no one round here talks about for fear of mispronouncing.

There, all of you. A level playing field.

Pupil

Across the gulf that separates from me
a woman who has chosen never to be seen
in colour, feel the street sun on her skin
or speak the language of her face and limbs
to anyone but family – who says
her male creator made her shameful,
that she is her father's property
and that all other men must see her sexually –

across the desk, the books, the centuries
Zainab gives me no choice
but to bore between the slit, deeper, longer
into her eyes than I have anyone's.
She has me look a lover's look.

Providence

I have not stumbled down a street in Haiti
with only half the skin on my back.
I have not been taken out of school
and taught to use an AK47 on my family.

I have not spent my adulthood locked up
for a crime I did not do.
I have not been given HIV
from a contaminated blood transfusion.

I have not eked my three-year life out
eating wallpaper. I have not handled methadone
or strapped on explosives.

I have not got God. But I have got to fifty-three
and walked through Chapeltown
and known, and sometimes known.

The small print

If I could give something
to all the beggars I've passed by, I'd give
the time of day, eye contact and food –
but would want to see them eat it.

To which someone will say
what right have you
to put conditions on your gift?
Just give. It's up to them
what they do with it.

And I
but what are scriptures if not conditions
on the otherwise amazing, rashly unconditional gift
of love?

August evening

In each drive, cars splay like trump cards.

Gardens darken, their flowers dropped
like children's on a walk.

Smells of lighter fuel and burning flesh
waft from patios.

Along the street, two girls in red football shirts
consider growing up.

In rooms now emptying of all but lone grandparents,
Corrie wheedles to its closing bars.

Nobody is watching.

No desert

A voice said: "It is no desert."
                – Stephen Crane

In Greenock by the Clyde there is a gap in the tenements, concreted
to keep out grass and sealed at the back by a high wall. To be there
is to stand at the bottom of a damp cardboard box – except that from
the middle of the patch a rusty spring pokes up a small metal seat
and equine head with handle-ears – too tough to call a toy, too small
– it would be small even indoors, even in a play pen – to call a ride.
The spring thrusts through the paving like a cartoon fist as if to say
Be a child then – two minutes! It sits there adrift on its concrete sea.
If it had friends, ever – an elephant to climb into, a monkey see-saw
– there are no scars. The seat remembers it was red and yellow once,
and in the wind sometimes trembles for a toddler.

Attitude

Made in England, for my sins I bear this image of you: this marriage
of words and geography which is more than green hills, greyness or London tat,
more than the union flag, tea, or that outdated sense of some great place in the world,
this print of you, England – which is not even you but you and your neighbours,
limpers bound in a tetchy three-legged race – branded like MADE IN TAIWAN
on the back of my mind, a bit of residual DNA I'm not sure how to use:

this scar of you as a backward E or battered pound sign, which is an L and Latin
so part of you as well, and therefore me; this body image which is, oddly, mine too,
of a flailing, ectomorphic, many-limbed old goat: your back to Scandinavia,
rump mooning at the Lowlands, sitting on France, Kent protruding like a cushion
from one surprisingly fat flank as you drool over Ireland, crumbs tumbling
from your beard, making a clumsy pass while looking incorrigibly past

at what you hope's your main chance. In geography, history; in history, your future
as ageing hack, satyr at a typewriter, aiming some tired apologia at your tireder muse.
Conceding what? Your neediness? How without Scotland you'd be headless,
armless without Wales, spineless without the north? Or how in the right light
you can look heraldic: *caprus, sejant erect*. Your heart a Mersey beat, your capital
a pelvic ache, how well the map catches you. Catches us, in fact.

Coast

They call it paradise, this land
that bled us dry – fanning
our burnt-out pride. But paradise

is for the dead. Let them try
as we did, squandering their young muscle
damming, digging trenches, laying drains –

let them winch nags up cliffs
or starve, wrestle mudslides, drought and flood –
and in a few years let them sicken

of the same few family names,
congenitally careworn faces.
Let them cultivate their feuds

in the same dog-stinking village haunts,
under the same peeling paint.

They call it paradise, this ache
of blue-white sky and mountain,
raising their eyes from pools and paperbacks –

then step out young, sun-stunned,
more wealth in their backpacks
than our hearths ever saw. So let them buy

our ruinous old barns and let us go –
up along the valley over that first col
whose angles spell out life and money

clear as Hollywood. We will find a land
that does not fight us. Mind your backs.
We will phone. We will send money.

Let us pass. Let them
make those stony fields pay.

Kingfisher on a tram

Eleven wonders

1 Snow.

2 At around seven, your first
bluebell wood. From then on, however far you travel
there will never be another.

3 The fact that you do travel, far.
4 That those huge metal slugs take off and float
over seas of cloud few humans saw till now,
but 5 that you have.

6 Winged flight of all kinds – a bird's vulnerability
weighed against that gift.
7 That all things distant go on moving and sounding
without you.
8 How a wound heals: its ministering armies.

9 Infinitudes of scale, both ways.
10 The sea – a certain haziness before that grey blur glimpsed
between hills parting like curtains on a show
to which all these
are mere overtures.

11 Snow.

Lumbricus Rex

Upon my belly I shall go, proudly. A stately retinue
unto myself, no hole or palace barred me, I shall proceed
at ease through private studded corridors – or else
encased in grit, shall lie with it, pulsing, rippling, alive.

At once tongue, finger, penis, nipple – what more is there?
My soul a gut, I shall have more yet: my own self to love,
my kind to meet and feed at death – but, half immortal,
each thrill of heat, dust, ice and flood till then to taste,
more dazzled by their spectrum than by sensed space or light.

Seismically tuned, my body's length a flexible antenna,
time, too, will be mine to apprehend. Lowest of the low,
knowing salvation and damnation, I shall fear nothing.
Bow down, world, to me. I shall be god of earth.

Kingfisher on a tram

After a while they start to annoy you
perched on every pondside information board,
common as unicorns,

so you add them to your life's quests
and weekend treks to willowy pools
where a man in a cap has just seen one
just a minute ago

and you trek home having seen nothing
but a man in a cap
and you blame yourself for being bad
at looking until at last, at last

a whacking great blue bruiser
of a thing, scruffy as a brickie mixing cement
sits or rather stands a stone's throw from you
long enough for you to believe in unicorns –

and years later thanks to this
you register the next split-second biro streak
along the grey canal past Matalan

that makes that instant click,
that vision lifelong, Meadowhall Elysian,
your tattooed ticket-girl an angel and your tram
a barge of burnished gold.

Home

That house was ours, once. I knew your ancestors.
Shy yellow wagtails, not of that century or this, they'd land
to pick their way across the grass then fly on.
Birdsong, here, was all we heard for years.

You are not afraid of us, exactly, either.
Each time we near, you flit reluctantly
a few feet further – still within sight but tolerant,
as if not wanting to offend guests.

Five or six times you do this,
staking your claim from each new post
till near the lane you tire of the game
and fly away for good.

Still, it is your domain – the fields, the dandelions
your inheritance, not mine.

On the map

Once it was a quiet road, a lane
whose sapling borders could be seen through
as you dawdled the half mile down to Wordley's shop,
a Mars Bar in your mind's eye,
sixpence and a 1919 penny in your hand.

Once but not every summer
the ice-cream van from Stoke,
its driver on a mission, would lumber up the hill,
park on the first bend and rev, raffishly,
Popeye the sailor man electrifying us.

Once but not every few years a siren,
real but unreal, would arrest our dreams
and have us window-staring through the dark
to where we guessed the road went.
You felt the whole village there too,

men wavering on steps, uncertain
whether to set off and know the worst
(somebody someone knew, no doubt) or stay
well out of it, that old longing for the kind of news
you could be named in safely
flaring like a wound.

Presence

Birthdays and Christmases, you used to make our presents.
Late at night you'd be outside somewhere sawing, planing, soldering –
a dolls' house for me, shoe-box square and got in through the flat roof,
a grey Mobil garage for my brother. A wooden sledge with runners
which went rusty, so heavy it just sank in the snow. A creaky swing.

We were unimpressed. They never matched the bought things
we'd had in mind. After bed I'd hear you talking through design points
with mum and sometimes, on cold afternoons, I'd come into the shed
and peer deep into the paraffin heater, loving its ring of flame
and purple fumes. Hoping for nothing, but that you would turn round.

The Rainy Day Book

What do you owe your parents? Forbearance.
Learning how not to complain but wait patiently,
not always knowing quite what the wait was for.

Everything comes to those who wait, you said –
and taught us, air-raid fashion, the ways. Reading.
Alphabet games like *Town and Country*. Taking turns
at drawing folded sections of fanciful characters.
Puzzle-book mazes. Join the dots.

As now, with the little I know, I try to picture
how each of you ever got from your stony childhoods
to each other, the wedding car, house to house,
hurt to hurt – to those long last nights, last hours
of waiting, playing *I spy* in the dark.

Hush hush

The switch is pressed on quietly, as if only its click
and not the glare could wake a nine-year-old.
Breath held, you unshut one eye.

>She is not your grandmother.
>People can marry twice.

'Granny' smells smoky, has ink lines for eyebrows,
wears lipstick *but no make up, dear*
and lots of clothes. A cardigan, a tie-waist dress

unbuttoned and slithered out of.
A knee-length petticoat with ribbon straps
and lace round the bust or bosom is it called.

>She never told Mum important things
>about girls growing up.

Big necklace and tiny watch
are off, rattled down somewhere.

Now, breathing more heavily,
the corset. Pale, bobbly flesh rolls
over its fish-paste pink, the pink of bald dolls,

false limbs – a bomb site frontage
of panels, tapes, loops, buttons, hooks and eyes,
suspenders.

>Grandpa was her lodger in the war, you heard,

but she had 'problems with her nerves'.

Thick stockings, unhitched, peel off
her legs, blancmangey. Veined. Are those
her nerves?

When Mum was seventeen she went out and bought herself
a bra.

So many things you mustn't talk about. Eye by eye
the bodice, unhooked,

                      sighs apart.

For what we are about to receive

Born in the fifties, our second-hand mindsets
leapfrogged back to the war and the one before that
and before that to Victoria, whose craggy silhouette
came with us sometimes to the sweet shop.

Queens you had to keep asking God to save
but Britannia who sat behind her would stand up
for us. Great aunts and grandmothers aped both
and at sixty graciously accepted cameo roles

in which they loured, shook sticks like tridents
and passed round fish paste sandwiches and scones
from doileyed stands, while we were given
Blackie's Children's Classics – Copperfields

and Eyres and Twists, abridged – to teach us
that as children we belonged in prison
or on the streets, that we had escaped slavery
and disease by the skin of our century,

should be grateful for our plateful and eat it all
may the Lord make us truly thankful.

No anaesthetic

1966. Ten years old
and I have got myself
to Bazeley Road dentists.

In the waiting room,
the sound of roadworks. That picture
of a boy in a dress with an apple.
Picasso, it had said.

Pushed back in the black chair now
I can see frosted glass, part of a roof
and one of those chimney-top things
that look like fat pigeons.

The woman revs her drill.
Exide, says the light in my face.

I do not have holes in my teeth
but she is about to make some.

I am to be punished
for sweets I have not eaten
but have thought about.

There is no one else here,
but I sort of think
there should be. A nurse

or something.

Twyfords, says the sink
I spit into.

Behind *The Turnip Harvest*

One Saturday we went inside
the Pickerings' – our semi neighbours.
Perched on their mustard settee
on our best behaviour, we sipped tea
in their front room, which was ours

inside-out, with the same criss-cross
wooden knick-knack rack but strange
ornaments and more furniture. And
they were croakier and even more
wrinkled here than outside. But kind.

Belle and Jack. Polyphotos of their son
Dennis who was working at Ferranti
in blue rompers. Embassy Regal
smoke climbed the Vymura trellis.
I took it all in, eating a lemon puff.

From then on, when their door slammed
you knew if you stepped through
our Rowland Hilder where you'd stand.
After the last strains of our *Doctor Who,*
their telly's alien kazoo made more sense.

Coasting

Sometimes momentarily
you're back there doing Geography,
the rows of pine tables warm,
the long room Thursday-stuffy
and the strip lights bright
against the outside blur
of brick and sodium, the looming fog
cocooning, bandaging,
erasing Manchester

to leave a kind of no man's land
of safety in the *Philip's High School Atlas*
open at Peru, Australia, The Great Lakes
with their oyster edges to be traced,
ink pens coaxed
towards that blissful payoff
with a flat blue crayon. That frill –
that made the exercise book
look three dimensional.

So easy then, it seemed, to sail
above the fog to lands of clarity,
neat blue boundaries
which sloped off evenly
to clear blue seas.
Time and a steady hand
all you'd need
to make the whole world safe.

Spell

All day long the fog has clung,
the fog has clung all day.
Carry me far away from here,
oh carry me far away.

All night long the wind has raged,
the wind has raged all night.
Carry me far away from here,
into the deadcalm light.

All day long the rain has drummed,
the rain has drummed all day.
Carry me far away from here,
oh carry me far away.

All night long the snow has swirled,
the snow has swirled all night.
Sweep me up and carry me off,
astonishing world in white.

Meanwhile

We were married on the twenty-sixth of April, nineteen-eighty-six,
a day when weeks of inauspicious grey gave way to a benign blue sky
and sunshine warm enough for guests to feel good about their flimsy clothes
and pose with real smiles for photographs against the spring-leaved trees.

Unsure of God we'd opted for a registrar and over cynics' quips
about the place being like a cinema got through our vows
and twenty hours later found ourselves in Portugal,
our Opel Corsa trundling past giant cacti to that villa ringed by citrus trees,
their fragrance on the breeze
which waltzed a sheet of dusty newsprint to our door.

We joked about our day being global news
but made out only place names – somewhere called Chernobyl –
from the Portuguese.

Later, in bed, holding our new rings to the filtered lemon light
we thought about our future and agreed that somehow – weatherwise at least –
we had been blessed.

Hear

as you surface to torpid half-darkness
this tide that has swept you towards these small hours:
this unsteady current you're no longer part of
unsettling the windows, partitions and doors.
Hear whitewater eddies of sirens and horns,
shutters and motors, brakes and exhausts –
a screech here, a slam there, a van roaring off,
a ringtone. An air lock. A snorer. A cough.

Corridor fumblings, footsteps and keys,
a street-level quarrel, a sweeping machine.
The wail of a freight train, the hum of a plane,
the answering thrum of a plate glass pane.
A haggling cabbie, bags slapped on the kerb,
the clack of stilettos. A dog disturbed.
An underground rumble, an overhead click.
Down on the river, the boom of a ship.

The trump of an artic lumbering past
a ruminant bin van, a grumbling bus.
A shudder of plumbing, a fan coming on.
Police helicopters. What sounds like a gun.
A lorry reversing, a hydraulic hiss,
a trolley, a pulley, the swish of a lift.
A snarl-up of scooters, a few seconds' calm –
then a drunken invective. A wayward alarm.

A hooter, a heater, a complicit knock,
a gobbet of laughter. The chime of a clock.
Rising, subsiding and fading away,

a snippet of music. The chink of a tray.
Merging and submerging, layer on layer
as far and beyond what the ear can hear –
a tide so insistent, pitched and profound
you could sleepwalk into its depths and drown.

Meeting Baudelaire

I
The cracked bell

It is bitter, yet sweet, during long winter nights
to hear, by the fire's smoky sputters and spits
recollections from far away slowly arise
through the carillon singing of bells in the mist.

O fortunate, vigorous, full-throated bell
who, age notwithstanding, stands solid and spry,
like a faithful old soldier on guard at the tent
who fiercely, religiously, raises the cry.

My own soul is cracking – and when, bowed by care,
she would have her songs people the frosty night air,
it seems that her weakened voice now brings to mind

the wounded death-rattle of one left behind
at a pool, by a pile of the dead, whose blood spreads
as the soul's efforts play out, unseen and immense.

II
Spleen (1)

Pluvius, irked by the entire city,
spills cold rain from his urn in dismal waves
over the wan inmates of next door's graves
and – into the suburbs – grim mortality.

My cat, on the tiles to claw himself a litter,
restlessly flexes his meagre, mangy pelt.
Some old poet haunts the dripping gutter,
his voice a ghost's, susceptible to cold.

The great bell clamours as a sputtering log
pipes in falsetto to the wheezing clock,
while from a rancid pack of playing cards

– a bloated old crone's deadly last bequest –
the queen of spades and dapper jack of hearts
trade murky tales of loves long turned to dust.

III
Confession

Once – just once – my lovely, gentle friend
you laid your smooth arm softly on my own.
(That memory's impression still, undimmed,
lights up the dark recesses of my soul.)

The hour was late. The full moon glimmered
like a new medal, spreading wide her beams
as night in its solemnity like some great river
over sleeping Paris, streamed.

Along the houses, under entranceways
a few cats padded, furtive, ears alert,
or like familiar shadows slowed their pace
to ours – unhurried fellow travellers.

Then suddenly, from that frank closeness
set free by the night's pale clarity –
from you, whose vibrant, rich persona
transmits only radiant gaiety –

from you, clear and joyous as a fanfare
in the sparkling dawn – a plaintive note
escaped: a strange uncertain tone
at once unsteady, falling, faltering

like some ill-favoured, shambling, squalid child
whose shamefaced family had long sought
to hide her from the censure of the world
by shutting her in secret in some vault.

This poor angel – you – half sang, half cried
'that nothing in this world's a certainty
and that however artfully disguised
the human ego gives itself away;

how it's a hard life being a working girl,
the dancer's routine posturings banal:
beneath her wild abandon she is cold,
her smile mechanical;

and that to build a life on hearts is mad
when beauty, love and all things fall apart
until Obscurity hoists up his hod
and carts the lot off to Eternity!'

I've often called back that enchanted moon,
that limpid, languid silence, and that stark
disclosure whispered, chillingly,
at the confessional of the heart.

Play

Exceedingly good cakes

They'd set the belt that bit too fast
to keep you at it sorting one each colour
you could hardly call them flavours
to a tray flinging them in like some casino
dreamt up by the Brothers Grimm
half eight to six except when things went wrong
and you got only yellows or just empty cases
or the filling fell off-centre gluing
every pastry moon to the conveyor
and you'd grab for knives or bits of cardboard box
and lunge to scrape them off and get the blobs
stuck clown-like down your overalls and toss
the scraped-off gunge into a paper sack
which overfilled and burst onto the floor beside you
which you had to clean as well
till someone bold would yell out stop
stop STOP the belt and they just might
and Kenny Everett would intercede
or not and you'd just muddle through
until you stepped outside deoveralled
and demob-capped for home and blinked,
the night sky full of jam tarts.

Saturday ghazal

Do you want to do second break Faye
Mrs Phillips is off with a migraine can I help you

I can't do first I've got the Parlophone rep
at half one what time d'you call this can I help you

Dust these racks will you Debbie they're filthy
scratched has she got a receipt can I help you

Bambi it's on order should be here Wednesday
record storage cases over there can I help you

There's a cream cake under the till for you
what a wino watch him did you smell can I help you

Do you know who sings it twenty-five past five
and they're still coming in can I help you

Somebody shut those doors for god's sake
haven't they got homes to go to sorry we're closed now

How many times have I told you Julia
to put the Queen's heads in this way round

Winfield Ruled

Between WE ARE CLOSING and WE ARE CLOSED
we press cold noses to the glass, sniffing at the past.
This paper white-out draws us in a way that lately
double doors and all that red and white busyness did not.

Inside stands a four year-old with sixpence among trays
of cut-throat Christmas baubles, notepads and *Tiny Tears*.
Down the street she's not keeping up with Dad's answer
to *how can such big blocks of chocolate be so cheap?*

There's my grammar-school friend Frances enthroned
at her Saturday job till in Piccadilly Gardens, *Europe's largest
Woolworths*, saying she'll leave us soon to work there full time.
There! By the steps where half Manchester first kissed –

and where later *Evening News* photographers caught limbs
flailing between smoke and window grilles.
Foam-filled furniture, pre-sprinkler valves, the killer.
Ten people and an era dead.

Then me again, queuing with my last ever Woolies purchase
and – as lavatory brushes aren't things you hold for long –
smalltalking with the next woman, also buying one.
Great minds think alike the opener, no doubt.

We stood about where on the lanes of dull wood laminate
those dusty racks now wait between a pair of captive staff,
one phoning someone, while behind her two *Coca-Cola* logos
tangle over bare chiller cabinets, like graveyard worms.

Christmas
is
coming

thundering
towards you like an Argos
juggernaut and between wanting
to shrink yourself to a grain of polystyrene
packaging and wanting to give shops another chance
and go with the flow of the lights and glitter and late night forays
in drizzly dark and wanting to buy stuff for yourself and wanting to throw up
everything for a mouldy caravan on the shores of Loch Tralee but having first
to nip to Sainsbury's for some sprouts and finding the streets a snarled-up circuit-board
of everybody nipping and shutting off damn Jo March's Christmas won't be Christmas without
and pondering the presumption of buying the slightest little thing for another adult and wanting
to ban Santa in favour of Father Christmas and wanting every child in the world to have a stocking
with a tangerine in and giving every person you love the ultimate symbol of how you love them
while wanting to say to relatives no we are not a hotel buy your own turkey clean your own toilet
be your own taxi and wanting to give to the Salvation Army and join in with their ding dong merrily
and make lists of who you should give cards to what a waste of forests but so are Christmas trees
and the needles end up everywhere and the trimmings bear the snot of four generations
of your family's kids and the baubles these days have got fatter like those massive tins
of Quality Street that used to be a tenth the size and the tin might be useful
but it never is and between all this you need to have a clearout
sort out cupboards sort out what you feel what you believe
before it's January and you're full but empty
as a diary and a cats calendar
you'll take to
charity.

Mooning

What is it with poets and the moon?
Page after page down every century
they think they are the first to spot
it's like a face, a cheese, a fruit,
a fingernail, a foetus or whatnot.

Then when they've clocked their own gog-eyed
amazement it's their children's – trying to catch the thing
and pin it down. Look, it can't be done.
I won't quite say you're wasting breath
but if it could, it would have been by now

and meanwhile, time is getting on.
The window's open, cold is rushing in and
you've got stuff to sort – papers, bills (gas bills) to pay.
Here, behind you, now and sneaking by
is Life on Earth. Come in

before you catch your death.
The moon is pale, it's silver yes, a bit
mysterious maybe. It's round/it's flat,
it's real/it's not. So what? Let's face it,
once you've seen one moon,

The wrong room

I really like this. Although...I'm not quite sure that I understand it.

But in a way that doesn't matter. I mean, we don't have to understand *everything*, do we?

No of course – I like being made to think. And I love the way he's used the 'e' sounds – E and c.

Keeps the rhyme to a minimum...very clever.

It's so economical – yet there's quite a lot to take in. Maybe you could have a line break somewhere, instead of punctuation? That 'equals' doesn't add anything, does it?

Yes, that would work. Take out the equals and have no punctuation at all, you mean?

The more you read this the more you see in it. I just wonder if you really need –

Actually, I wasn't sure about the rhyme. Thought it was maybe a bit – obvious. I wondered if you could change one of those letters to something non-rhyming? Tone it down a bit.

Not the c though. That's a really lovely allusion, to the sea. Reminds me of *Dover Beach*.

Yes, and it's the only concrete image, isn't it? We need that to hold on to.

Oh, I must have misunderstood – I didn't read it like that at all. I read it as 'see' – a bit of authorial intervention. 'E = m, see.'

Well it can hold both those meanings, surely? Just one tiny niggle though – if you're having a line break, won't that make the next M a capital?

Oh no, leave it. It's more modern, lower case.

My computer does capitals anyway. I've not worked out how to stop it.

That's Microsoft for you. You should get a Mac.

Expensive way to get rid of capitals!

We used to have some lovely holidays, by the sea...

Er, can we get back to the poem? What does anyone think about the ending?

Good   ?

I liked it – but. Well, this is just nit-picking, but perhaps you could lose that last little bit? I mean, by the time we get there we all *know* it's squared, don't we? You don't need to spell it out.

It was the start that bothered me more. That E feels a bit like padding – just getting into the subject. Wouldn't it be stronger without it?

So take out the E, and the ending?

And the rhyme – and just have M, and maybe another letter that doesn't rhyme.

Right! Time's moving on.

No, just m – lower case.

OK. Anyone anything else for Albert?

The deep

Inside the bottle on the windowsill
under the surface of its standing water
cars and buses swim by upside down
in a parabola within its fisheye lens.

Up to the front in turn they lunge,
swell up, then shrink back down and off:
red mail van, orange access bus,
unmarked white transit topped with ladders.

Between and beyond, along the pavement
from right to left a woman in a plum coat
passes the rugby pitch where, almost
too small to make out, four seagulls

and a crow practise manoeuvres
as a lad in pale blue jeans sits on the wall
by the bus stop drumming his trainers,
unaware of his underwater life.

Ray

There's someone in the aquarium
trapped behind the pane, mouthing *Under this mortal coil, chum,*
you and I are the same.

From the other side of the great divide
in cerebral collision, a moment of mutual knowledge brings
primordial recognition.

From a bodiless bloodless flattened face
it looks me in the eye, mouthing *Here but for fate go you, mate –*
but there but for fate go I.

Twins at the dawn of creation
our ways have since diverged, you to the realms of fire and earth,
me blissfully submerged.

To you a clumsy finless fate,
to me a dancer's ease. To me the fabulous birthday suit,
to you the snaggled weeds.

Your fins extruded to useless fronds,
your face on a wobbly knob, I'm sorry evolution
did such a dodgy job.

From here in this watery paradise
where food just comes to me – who'd be in your shoes, pal,
for all the fish in the sea?

The glass ship

And into the offing there came
a ship-sized, shipshape galleon all the sea colours of glass
from its sixty-foot hull of portholes, bulwarks and gunnels
all an impossible iceberg blue to its grey-green sails
translucent in the sun, its tinkling crows' nest, futtock shrouds,
struts and mainmast, topgallant mast and topmast stays,
its mizzenmast, jib and boom, its ratlines, spankers, binnacles,
hawsers, strops and lanyards invisible almost against the spray,
to their pennants tapering into a wind edging everything shorewards
to waver becalmed for an instant before sudden storm clouds arose
and hurled pennants and lanyards strops and hawsers binnacles
spankers ratlines boom jib mizzenmast topmast stays
topgallant mast mainmast struts and futtock shrouds crows' nest
sails gunnels bulwarks portholes and hull to the rocks
to be shattered and scattered to figments sifted to shingle
and crunched underfoot by onlookers
looking to cart off what they could.

Then sometimes you'll think

of greenhouses – which are not green but transparent, not named for themselves
but for a quality they might engender: their panes flyblown, crusty – frames crying out
for a lick of something tender, like the care their charges get.

And you may think of the word dicotyledons for seedlings' two first leaves –
those small arms waving *look, world, we are here* – forgetting too soon
the disintegrating glass womb that they still need.

And you may think of greenhouses' secret armpit smell and damp peaty hug,
surprised how something so weak-looking can contain such heat, comforting at first
then coaxing you to put down roots, mutate into some freak vegetable;

and of their mess – the runtish tools. Yogurt pot archive. Margarine museum.
Plastic bottles with 'harmful' crosses. Something blackish brown, in a jar. On the floor
a once-red watering can, now faded to old lady pink. The pink of that geranium.

And you may think of how they all need attention. Think of old ladies – their shared air
of resignation, life interrupted, things unsaid: trays and eccentric crockery set out
as if somebody longed-for has turned up and then, as unexpectedly, just left.

Date

Strange how we've both dressed up for this
when we always used to dress down.
You can't fool me: that's a flak jacket
under your shirt, or a cushion –

and some crafty make-up bod
has roughed up your skin, added lines
to your eyes, bad teeth – and you're wearing
one of those bald wigs.

But then here's me in this granny mask,
wrinkly pink and purple gloves,
crimped body suit, sprinkling of moles
and talc all over my hair.

And look – we've both brought glasses
to read between the lines.

Play

Sooner or later they will have
the conversation about hands.

You've got [such and such] hands
one will say, watching the other
raise a cup, spoon, book, paper –
yours are/mine are/look/let's see.

Side by side then palm to palm,
skin to skin, finger to finger
tip to tip, they'll size up shape,
colour, muscle – scrutinise nails.

An aftertouch of heat, moisture,
pressure – then the world will shift
on its axis and the light slant
ever so slightly differently.

Wheeeee

Watching Filey funfair's Mega G-Force –
the one which straps kids into firing lines
to swish them up and down for three full minutes –

and other gewgaws to remind them they're alive –
inverters, *chair-o-planes* and the *Black Hole*,
where you're on some kind of switchback
but only your innards tell you what –

I think of the buried dead – each strapped
in their own black hole, backs to the turning earth,
white-knuckled, too cool to whimper – facing space
for the longest ride of their lives.

Voltage

Blackpool, you old goat, lay down your wet-look mac
for the raggle-taggle trippers jaywalking your tramlines
this September Saturday as chips, beer, sweat and diesel
on the breeze bite rock hard under black skies back at last
and nights stitched up in lights, summer's come-on ditched
for winter's electricity. Khaki under sodium the bedding plants
parade along the prom to Ginn Square past a policeman
somewhere laughing, laughing, laughing as the pier in bling
and heels throws her secrets to the sea, which bites its lip.